Finally! A Concise And Comprehensive Divorce Guidebook!

Learn from the experts and the 20/20 hindsight of hundreds of other divorces.

The divorce rate in the U.S is close to 50% and in the State of California; it is close to 60%. In this easy-to-read and informative Itty Bitty Book, Kathy Costas and Evan Miller provide an essential roadmap to help you successfully navigate the divorce process.

The 15 tips in this book will guide you through every phase of the divorce process and provide you with the resources to make the best decisions during the worst of times. You will learn:

- How to gather the important financial information and put together the perfect divorce team.
- How to make smart decisions regarding the family home and other key assets.
- How to establish a parenting plan and communication ground rules.

Pick up a copy of this powerful book today and experience the confidence in knowing you have the tools you need to survive and thrive during and after your divorce.

Your Amazing Itty Bitty® Divorce Handbook:

15 Essential Tips to Help You Make the Best Decisions During the Worst of Times

Kathy Costas, CDFA®
Evan Miller, CDFA ®/CFP

Published by Itty Bitty® Publishing
A subsidiary of S & P Productions, Inc.

Copyright © 2019 Kathy Costas, Evan Miller

All rights reserved. No part of this book may be reproduced or transmitted in any form or by any means, electronic or mechanical, including photocopying, recording or by any information storage and retrieval system, without written permission of the publisher, except for inclusion of brief quotations in a review.

Printed in the United States of America

Itty Bitty Publishing
311 Main Street, Suite D
El Segundo, CA 90245
(310) 640-8885

ISBN 978-1-950326-25-9

This book is dedicated to my children, Emily, Nick and Hailey, who are my reason for being and to all of the other angels in my life who carried me through my divorce and continue to love and guide me.

Kathy

This book is dedicated to my wonderful wife Melissa and joyful son Will. You fill my days and heart with happiness and love.

Evan

Stop by our Itty Bitty® website to find to additional interesting information regarding financial planning for divorce.

www.IttyBittyPublishing.com

Or visit Kathy and Evan at

http://fmbdivorcefinancialplanning.com

or reach out to them directly at

Kathy@fmbwealth.com or Evan@fmbwealth.com

To go directly to our website use the code below:

Introduction

This book is designed to serve as a guide so that you can benefit from the mistakes of the many divorcing couples who have come before you. It is just the "20/20 hindsight" everyone wishes they had at the beginning of their divorce.

This book is for you if:

- You don't know how to make the best first steps.
- You are feeling alone and overwhelmed by the financial decisions that need to be made and the steps that need to be taken to secure your financial future.
- You are worried about protecting your children's lifestyle and financial future.
- You are afraid your spouse has an unfair advantage in financial matters.
- Your current financial advisor is not a Certified Divorce Financial Analyst, CDFA®.

In most cases, divorce is a marathon not a sprint. It involves twists and turns along the way and a few hills you may not have seen coming. Even on a smooth course, you need the right preparation for each step and a strong support team. Having the right information and expert professionals behind you will save you time and money and get you to a much better position at the finish line.

Whether it's deciding to keep or sell the house, or determining a fair division of assets, the tips in this book are designed to help. We understand the emotions that surround these decisions, but with some guidance and expert advice, the right choices can be made.

Our 15 essential tips will help you:

- Build a divorce team you can trust.
- Gather the important financial information.
- Set goals and determine the best settlement.
- Create a sound financial strategy for your future.

Sometimes taking that first step is the hardest. This book will take you by the hand and help get you on your way. If you need additional information or resources, go to our website at http://fmbdivorcefinancialplanning.com or reach out to us directly at Kathy@fmbwealth.com or Evan@fmbwealth.com.

Tip #1
Where Do I Start?

Hunt and Gather Your Financial Information. This first step will help you begin to see what you are entitled to and what your future financial picture might look like. If you do it well it will also save you time and money with an attorney or mediator. You should try to gather and organize all of your financial records from the past 3 years including:

1. Personal and business tax returns
2. Latest pay stubs for both of you
3. Banking and credit card statements
4. Mortgage statements
5. Investment account statements
6. Retirement account statements, including IRAs, 401ks, Pensions or other company plans
7. Deferred compensation plans
8. All insurance policies and annuities
9. Descriptions of employee benefits
10. A list of large property items
11. A description of any debt
12. Any completed financial affidavits – listing of assets, liabilities, income and expenses for both of you

Things to Consider When Putting This Information Together:

Knowledge is power. Now is the time to become informed; that is the inspiration behind this sometimes daunting task!

- If in doubt, include anything with a $ sign.
- Start watching the mail and paying attention to any financial statements that arrive especially if you are not the one who usually deals with the money in your household.
- The more organized you are the easier it will be for your attorney to use this information to protect your interests.
- If you have property or assets that were owned prior to marriage, do your best to find a paper trail that can document how and when the asset was acquired and why it is separate property.

Tip #2
Be A Team Player

It doesn't matter if you will be playing tackle football or just a chess match with your spouse, you owe it to yourself and your family to create a team to support you through this process. Your team should include a legal expert (attorney or mediator), a therapist and a certified divorce financial planning expert.

1. As with any life changing decision, you should get at least two qualified opinions on the best way to settle your divorce.
2. Explore the option of mediation if you feel you can agree on the basics.
3. Spend the time and money up front on full expert consultations. Don't just rely on the recommendation of friends or family.
4. Choose this next legal "partner" wisely. Trust and communication will be key. This person will be representing you and your family's best interests and you may be working together for several months and possibly a few years.
5. Find a therapist you feel most comfortable with.
6. Your financial expert should be a Certified Divorce Financial Analyst®.

Things to Consider When Building Your Team:

- Each attorney or mediator has their own personality, style and strengths. Do your best to match the person and their firm with your case and your opponent.
- Mediation doesn't mean you agree on everything, just that you agree you don't want a judge deciding your future. This process is especially beneficial if you have young children together. You won't always be spouses, but you will always be parents.
- A Certified Divorce Financial Analyst®, (CDFA®) is a valuable resource. They must pass a series of exams on all financial aspects of divorce and can testify as an expert witness in court if that is necessary.
- Treat your first meetings with all of these experts like a job interview. Ask them about their experience, ask for a timeline and estimate of costs as well as a game plan and some "what ifs".
- Always rely on your friends and family for love and support, but not for legal or expert advice. Leave that to your qualified team members.

Tip #3
Money 101

All money is not created equal. Accurate valuations of all accounts are needed to determine what mix of assets is best for you. Start working with a CDFA® or other qualified divorce financial planner right away so you can learn about what you have and what you want.

1. Checking, savings and brokerage or investment accounts are usually the most liquid and easy to access and divide.
2. This is an important point if you will be needing extra cash to set up a new household, pay your attorney etc.
3. Retirement accounts such as IRAs & 401Ks are not considered as liquid. There are often penalties and taxes on money taken out.
4. Retirement accounts, while not always liquid, are a very valuable savings tool for the future.
5. A CDFA® or financial planner should review all investment accounts both taxable and retirement, to determine values, liquidity and future growth potential.

Things to Consider About Money and Divorce:

- While divorce is most often about the money, attorneys and mediators aren't qualified to give you financial planning advice. Attorneys go to law school, they are not financial planners. They will tell you what you are entitled to but not necessarily what you really want based on your future.
- Solid financial advice is especially important if you are not the "money manager" in your marriage or if your spouse is the owner of a business that supports your family.
- While you may not be a numbers person or have experience with investments, you owe it to yourself and your children to start educating yourself and most importantly working with an advisor you trust. You will be making decisions during the divorce that will impact the rest of your life.
- Divorce is a very emotional process. Treating it like a business decision is almost impossible. Rely on a trusted financial advisor to help make logical decisions with your money.

Tip #4
The Divorce Diet

In any divorce the "B" word, budget that is, should be used early and often. You wouldn't hire someone to remodel your kitchen without knowing what you could afford to spend and what part of the project was most important to you. Don't hire an attorney to remodel your life without having some idea what it might cost.

1. Keep in mind, a higher hourly rate does not necessarily equal a higher settlement or support number. It's more important to work with an attorney you trust and can communicate with.
2. A CDFA® can be instrumental in helping you determine what you can afford to spend and more importantly what is worth fighting, and spending, for.
3. Ask about different ways to get the information you and your lawyer need. If you can do the leg work instead of your lawyer, you'll save hundreds of dollars or more.
4. Now is the time to get your personal spending under control as well. See more about this under Tip #7.

Things to consider about your Divorce Budget:

- A lot of people lose weight without trying to during the divorce process. Unfortunately, without a budget to guide them, they also lose a lot of money they don't need to lose.
- Try to keep in mind that in a few years you will heal and start to move on. At that point the big picture will be much more important than the coffee maker you spent $3,000 fighting for.
- Taking depositions and hiring forensic accountants are usually the most expensive "add ons" to the divorce process. Make sure they are necessary to finding the answers you need.
- You may be told that you should treat this as a business deal. The problem is, it's not a business deal, it's your past, your present and your future.
- Hire an expert you trust to provide that logical analysis of your budget and do your best to listen to them.

Tip #5
Credit Where Credit Is Due

The one score you need to settle in your divorce is your Credit Score. Most of the focus in the divorce is on who gets what asset. Don't forget to figure out who owes what as well. While you're looking for hidden money, make sure you also look for hidden debt.

1. Pull your credit report from all three reporting agencies as soon as you decide to separate or divorce. A good free site is annualcreditreport.com.
2. It's important to account for all of these debts and determine if they are community or only belong to one of you.
3. Your overall FICO score is a good indication of your credit strength but keep in mind you have many FICO scores based on different formulas that are used for different purposes.
4. If you don't have any credit cards in just your name, now is the time to get one.
5. Don't close or cancel any joint credit cards that have a good credit history. That will erase all of the good history you have built. Just take one name off of the card.

Things to consider about your credit score:

- The misuse of credit can be used as a weapon in divorce when one spouse refuses to pay a mortgage or other debt. This can impact both of you for several years. Make sure you have confirmation that bills are being paid if you aren't the one paying them.
- Your ability to get credit before you are divorced but while you are separated, will be based on your household income which includes the income from both of you. That will change once you are officially divorced.
- If you are not the main wage earner, your credit score and history will be an even more important asset to you. From a rental application or mortgage application to getting a car loan, this score can make your future life easier or much more difficult.

Tip #6
The Kids Can Hear You

During the divorce, the parents need strict rules and firm limits. Divorce is a whole new territory in parenting. Consider meeting with a therapist at the beginning to lay the ground rules on communication with and around the kids. Words often become weapons in this battle and they will leave a lasting mark. You both need to be clear on the best way to avoid wounding your children.

1. What may seem like a dig at your spouse can actually be interpreted by a child as blame on them.
2. Even if you can't agree on anything else, do your very best to be a united front on this aspect.
3. No matter what their age, kids do NOT want to be involved in this process in any way. This is your stuff not theirs. Don't ask them to be a referee, shoulder to cry on or a spy. They will resent having that burden put on them.
4. Remember, by definition "family court" is charged with doing what's in the best interest of the children. Make sure your words and actions would fall in that category or you may suffer in court.

Things to consider about parenting during a divorce:

- Children come into the world with unconditional love for their parents. They are not wired to take sides. Don't try to make them. You would never want to be asked to choose one child over another. That is the same pain they will feel.
- Holding your tongue may take the greatest strength you've ever had to muster. But just like the small mother who lifts a car off of her child, you have the inner strength to do this. You will be saving their emotional life and your future relationship.
- Your kids should be off limits and never used as a bargaining chip. If that starts to happen, seek help immediately from a professional and get both of you back on the right track.

Tip #7
When One Becomes Two-Households That Is

If you're not a numbers person, you can always rely on your baking skills. Think of the money you have to run your household every month as a pie. Now you need to cut that pie into two pieces to represent the two households you will need to support going forward. This is the reality of divorce.

1. If custody will be 50/50, the goal of the court is to create two households with roughly equal funds available.
2. Based on simple math then, division not multiplication is what is used to arrive at those numbers. Understanding this at the beginning of the process will help guide your expectations and could save you from wasting attorney fees down the road.
3. Now is the time to get a good handle on your monthly expenses and what it takes to run your household.
4. Compromises will likely need to be made on both sides in order to make this math work. Do your best to work together so you can keep your overall costs down.

Things to keep in mind about creating two households:

- If you are not used to managing money this can feel overwhelming and scary. Rely on a CDFA® or other trusted advisor to help you track your expenses and manage costs. It will pay off during the process and get you started off on the right foot once the divorce is done.
- Work with a therapist to determine how to discuss your new budget with your children. If it's appropriate you can work with them to decide what expenses may have to be reduced. Sometimes having a choice can be more important to them than what they may have to go without.
- Even if there is more than enough to go around at the outset, make sure you don't rely on retail therapy for you or to win favor with your children. Money spent from the community can be charged back against you and you could end up owing money to your spouse.
- Most divorces cost more and take longer than you plan. Pace yourself and your spending so that you don't run out of steam or cash.

Tip #8
The Dissomaster - All New For 2019

Spousal support, child support and your tax return all mixed together. In California, the dissomaster is the tool that is used to dice and slice your household income into monthly spousal and child support numbers.

1. The goal of this program is to take the total income for both of you and divide it in two separate roughly equal incomes.
2. It is almost always used to determine the initial or temporary support order and then may be finetuned in order to determine the final support order.
3. Child support is not taxable to the recipient and is not a tax deduction to the payor. It can be adjusted upward from the guideline but not downward.
4. Spousal support is a very different story. In California it is calculated after child support and is subject to negotiation.
5. A big change in divorce law came into effect on 1/1/2019. Starting on this date for new orders, spousal support will no longer be a tax deduction to the payer and will not be taxable to the recipient. More on this change in Tip #11.

Things to keep in mind about the Dissomaster:

- This tool is only used in California. Other states use different methods to calculate both child and spousal support.
- Because this is just a computer program, the numbers it generates are only as good as the data used as an input. Make sure you and your attorney understand and agree with each line item before you agree to a support order the program generates.
- Keep in mind that it takes a large shift in custodial time and/or income in order to have a significant impact on the support order. Have your attorney run several different scenarios so you know your best and worst case.
- The final orders for spousal support from a judge are generally 15-20% lower than what the dissomaster spits out. There are several reasons for this, but just make sure you keep that fact in mind when you're negotiating or deciding whether or not to go to trial.

Tip #9
A Better Way Than Right Down The Middle

Typically, the method to divide assets in a community property state and often an equitable distribution state, is to split each community asset right down the middle. There are often much better ways to do this from a financial planning point of view.

1. Create an inventory of all assets, both community and separate. The separate assets you have could make certain community assets more or less valuable.
2. Work with your CDFA® or tax professional to make sure you know the tax implications of all assets before you enter into any negotiations (see Tip #3 for more on this).
3. Your tax bracket and financial needs will change during different phases of your life. Your CDFA® can create cash flow projections to make sure the assets you are negotiating for have the tax treatment and liquidity to best meet these needs.
4. Do your best not to be emotionally tied to one asset. This can happen with the family home. Evaluate what you are giving up for each asset you choose.

Things to keep in mind when deciding how to divide assets:

- Your assets may have different long-term values to each of you depending on your current and future earning capacity and separate property, for example. This often provides an opportunity to get creative in the division and make both of you better off in light of your post-divorce goals and needs.
- Like all of these crucial steps and decisions, knowledge is power. First determine your goals and needs during the different periods of your life, then make sure you understand what assets will best support them.
- There are a lot of variables to pull together, but your CDFA® or other qualified financial professional can use sophisticated financial projection software to explore different scenarios and determine what is best for you. This is the time to use your team.

Tip #10
What About Your Home?

Your home is filled with memories and emotions. For this reason, it is often a major point of contention during a divorce. Use your CDFA® to help you make the best decision about this asset. You don't want to fight for a home you can't afford to keep. You will lose twice.

1. Maintenance on a larger home can end up being an albatross. Do the cash flow analysis that includes property taxes, HOA fees, insurance, gardener etc. so you know whether you can afford to stay. You will also need a cash reserve set aside for unforeseen expenses or major repairs.
2. Determine the cost of alternative housing. It may be cheaper to stay in the house if you have a small mortgage.
3. One spouse can't just assume the mortgage from the other spouse. It is considered a refinance at current rates and with the full approval process.
4. Capital gains tax on the sale of the home is another major point to consider. If you have a lot of equity you will keep more of it if you sell the house when you are still both owners.

Things to keep in mind about your home:

- Many parents feel it is important to keep the house if there are children still living there. They are hoping to maintain some stability for the kids during a large life change. Just make sure this decision doesn't result in a huge financial strain and potential loss of the home a few years later.
- To help you determine your options, work with a trusted mortgage professional to see what you would qualify for. Many mortgage lenders will consider spousal and child support as income as long as the order has been in effect for 3-6 months and will continue for the next 3 years. There are also lenders who will calculate an asset depletion schedule if you receive a lump sum buyout or other large sum of cash or investments.
- Generally speaking children feel stability and comfort when both parents are calm, happy and not stressed about money. Use this as your guide when making the decision about the home.
- If you decide that selling the home is best for everyone, involve the children in selecting the next home. You might be surprised how excited they will get when they have an opportunity to pick their new room or neighborhood.

Tip #11
Spousal Support & The 2019 Tax Law

Alimony, maintenance and spousal support all mean the same thing. What is very different is the tax treatment of these payments beginning in January 2019. This tax treatment changes the amounts awarded and will result in different negotiations as attorneys look for creative ways to structure the payments.

1. The new law only applies to settlements entered on January 1, 2019 or later.
2. Prior to this change, spousal support was taxable income to the recipient and a tax deduction to the payor. The reason for the change is that the money that will be paid as support will be taxed at the higher rate of the higher wage earner.
3. From a negotiation point of view, this change makes a lump sum payment of support, which has never been taxable, potentially as attractive as an ongoing payment for both sides.
4. There are other ways to recreate this tax treatment through the settlement structure including using K-1 distributions for business owners for example. The goal is to increase the total amount of money available to both parties, not to the IRS.

Things to keep in mind about the tax law change and spousal support:

- While there has been a lot of press about this major change, it is not necessarily good or bad for you. Each situation is different with opportunities to create the best scenarios for you and your family.
- The change does mean there will likely need to be a more in-depth analysis by the financial professionals of the level of need for support as well as the income available to pay it.
- For couples over 59 ½ you may consider using retirement accounts for a support order. This type of account generates taxable income to the recipient and contributions are a tax deduction to the payor. This sets up an income stream that mimics the old tax treatment of spousal support. This type of solution should be evaluated carefully by your CDFA® and tax professional to determine the long- term effect for both of you.
- By making this payment tax neutral, there are more options to view your assets in terms of using them as potential sources of support. Your assets may be more reliable payment sources than your spouse.

Tip #12
Forensic Accountants And Other Specialists – Do You Need Them?

Much like a medical condition, the more complex the issues in the divorce, the more likely you will need additional specialists. The difficult part is being able to make an informed decision about the need to involve them and incur added costs.

1. The most common specialist is a forensic accountant. They are vital to establishing the value of a business as well as tracing funds if there is money moving from account to account. They are also used to trace separate property claims and to value more complex assets such as pension plans.
2. Another common specialist is the QDRO, Qualified Domestic Relations Order attorney. They specialize in creating the legal documents that divide 401ks, pension plans or deferred compensation plans.
3. If you are in a custody battle you may need to hire a custody evaluator. They are usually therapists who determine the best custody arrangement.
4. Vocational evaluators can be necessary to determine the income potential of a spouse.

Things to keep in mind about hiring specialists:

- The common misconception about forensic accountants is that they act as detectives to find hidden money. The reality is they use the information provided by each of you to create a financial snapshot.
- Private investigators act as detectives to gather information. They conduct asset searches to see if there is money that your spouse is hiding. They can also make sure you aren't being spied on by your spouse through your phone, computer, car or even cameras and microphones in your home.
- Another common misconception about forensics is that they give you financial advice. That is not at all their role. They give you a balance sheet that lists all of your assets and debts as of a certain date but they don't tell you which assets you want or what those assets will be worth in 5 or 10 years. That is the job of your CDFA®, another important specialist to include on your team in most circumstances.
- Don't be afraid to speak up and ask your attorney why you need a specialist. Make sure it isn't just part of their process. However, if necessary, you will likely be very glad you hired them.

Tip #13
No Such Thing As Forever With Spousal Support

Like marriage, there are no guarantees that spousal support will last forever. Even if there is no official end date to the order, circumstances can arise that reduce or end those payments.

1. A spousal support order is determined by the ability to pay, need for support, limits on the ability of the recipient to earn income, marital lifestyle, findings of domestic violence and several other factors. The death of either spouse causes an end to support as does remarriage, and in some cases cohabitation.
2. In many states, spousal support for a marriage of less than 10 years lasts for half the length of the marriage. For marriages longer than 10 years there is often no official end date, but certain changes can end it immediately or reduce it over time.
3. Increasingly, the courts are expecting both parties to be working toward financial independence without support.
4. There are also the unforeseen events such as job loss or disability of the payor that end or reduce support.

Things to keep in mind about spousal support orders:

- Most support orders are modifiable and can be changed when one party retires or changes jobs etc. Even a non-modifiable order is difficult to enforce if there is simply not enough money to pay.
- Don't try to spend up to the marital lifestyle number in an attempt to get more support. You will just end up depleting assets and you'll have less money in the end. You may also owe money back to the other spouse.
- No matter what the circumstance, it is important for you to make efforts to become financially self- sufficient or at least to provide a supplemental income source as a backup to a support order. Things happen in life and both spouses should do their best to protect their financial well-being.
- Becoming financially independent should be seen as a reward not a punishment. It will allow you to have complete freedom from your spouse and provide for a future that you design all on your own.

Tip #14
Ways To Secure Your Final Judgement

The final divorce judgement is just a piece of paper. You need to take steps to make it more powerful than that and to cover the "what ifs".

1. Life insurance should be part of any settlement that includes a child support order. The goal is to have a death benefit that is large enough to replace the support in case the payor passes away.
2. Disability insurance is another important support protection. Someone in their 40s is far more likely to be disabled than to die. This is especially important for certain professionals who rely on their physical capabilities to earn income.
3. If the settlement includes another ongoing payment obligation such as a note payable over time, be sure this obligation is made into a legal Note and both of you sign it. The Note should be secured by some other asset as well.
4. Don't be afraid to use a wage garnishment order to collect on a support order. It isn't difficult to set up and can actually be easier for both of you in that there is no need to write a check twice a month.

Things to keep in mind about securing your support order:

- With life insurance, ideally the policy should be stand alone, not through an employer so that it does not disappear if the job does. Also, the recipient of support should be added as a second notice so that if a premium isn't paid you will know before the policy terminates.
- Another great child support enforcement tool in California is the Department of Child Support Services. The DCSS will enforce a garnishment order and monitor all payments. They can seize other assets if support is not paid and best of all this service is completely FREE.
- You've worked so hard to get to a final agreement. Don't lose the value of all of that work by not completing these final steps. Family law court doesn't have as many enforcement tools as criminal court for example so you need to make sure you do all you can to get what is yours.
- A CDFA® is a great resource to help you with these final steps. The attorney's job is finished with the judgement. A CDFA® will help you move accounts and monitor payments and make sure all of the financial details are covered and secured. Take a breath and push through this last step with a CDFA® helping out. You'll be very glad you did.

Tip #15
If You Have Children, It's Never Final

You won't always be spouses but you will always be parents. Make plans now and set expectations for the future that will help your whole family as you transition from one household to two.

1. The custody arrangement written into your settlement is based on the current ages of your children. As they get older and have different priorities and more rigorous school demands, try to agree to be somewhat flexible with your plans.
2. Work with a parenting coach to help you anticipate changes with your children and facilitate the flexibility that might be required. Communication will be key and since you will be living apart that can be more difficult.
3. Make a plan to cover expenses for the kids' activities. Consider funding an account each school year with an agreed amount and contribution percentage to cover these costs.
4. One of the biggest financial goals parents have is a college education. Make plans now and set financial targets so you are both clear about the expectations you both have.

Things to keep in mind about parenting after a divorce:

- There are apps such as www.2houses.com and www.ourfamilywizard.com that provide shared calendars and an email tool to help you work together. This can be another great way to keep the lines of communication open for parenting.
- Don't forget the final act of parenting that is creating an estate plan. You will need a trust to make sure your children are the recipients of your assets as well as a guardianship plan in case this transfer happens when they are young. It's not something you want to think about but once done, the peace of mind it will give you that you are taking care of your children forever makes it worth it.
- As time goes on and emotions fade, there will be graduations, weddings and births that you will both want to be a part of. Agree to work together as parents so you and your children can enjoy these milestones.

You've finished. Before you go…

Tweet/share that you finished this book.

Please star rate this book.

Reviews are solid gold to writers. Please take a few minutes to give us some itty bitty feedback.

ABOUT THE AUTHORS

Kathy Costas

Going through my own 6 year divorce inspired me to turn that bad experience into something good. I saw a big need for financial planning advice during and after divorce, and knew that was the way I could use my "lemons" to help others make "lemonade". I have found my passion and my purpose!

I started my career in financial services in 2008 and am now an Investment Advisor as well as a CDFA® or Certified Divorce Financial Analyst®. This credential allows me to provide solid financial planning advice in the context of divorce.

I use this education and my personal experience to serve as a compassionate guide to help clients successfully navigate the financial aspects of the divorce process. I am always working to learn more and be a great resource to clients.

I am the LA area Chapter Chair of the Divorce Alliance, a member of the Conejo Divorce Resource Group, and a presenter for the Second Saturday divorce group in Ventura County. I am also very active with the Cystic Fibrosis Foundation, and as a member of the local chapter of Dining For Women. My work can be exhausting and emotionally draining, but there is no greater reward in life than watching someone emerge from fear and sadness into confidence and happiness!

Evan Miller

Over the past 17 years as a Wealth Manager, I have found great joy in working with people I care deeply about and doing everything possible to have a positive impact on their lives.

In 2012 I was working with a client that was going through a divorce and discovered that there was a serious "void" in the divorce process leaving people to make important financial decisions that would impact every aspect of their future without any real guidance. I realized that I could help solve this and found my passion as a result.

As a CFP® and CDFA® or Cerified Divorce Financial Analyst, I have developed a process to help people determine their most important goals for the future and provide the tools to make financial decisions that put them in the best position to accomplish them. I have found tremendous fulfillment in seeing the impact this has on theirs and their children's futures.

I am also very active in my community as a Big Brother and support the charity P.O.R., an organization that helps support people and their families that are fighting pancreatic cancer.

I hope this book helps people find confidence and clarity to move forward in a positive direction.

If you enjoyed this Itty Bitty® book you might also like…

- **Your Amazing Itty Bitty® Fear-Busting Book** – Lucetta Zaytoun

- **Your Amazing Itty Bitty® Stress Reduction Book** – Denise Thomsom, CHC

- **Your Amazing Itty Bitty® Affirmations Book** – Micaela Passeri

Or any of the many Amazing Itty Bitty® books available on line.

www.ingramcontent.com/pod-product-compliance
Lightning Source LLC
Chambersburg PA
CBHW061305040426
42444CB00010B/2528